10/22

C0-DXC-497

Discarded By
Easttown Library

BIGGEST NAMES IN SPORTS

LAMELO BALL
BASKETBALL STAR

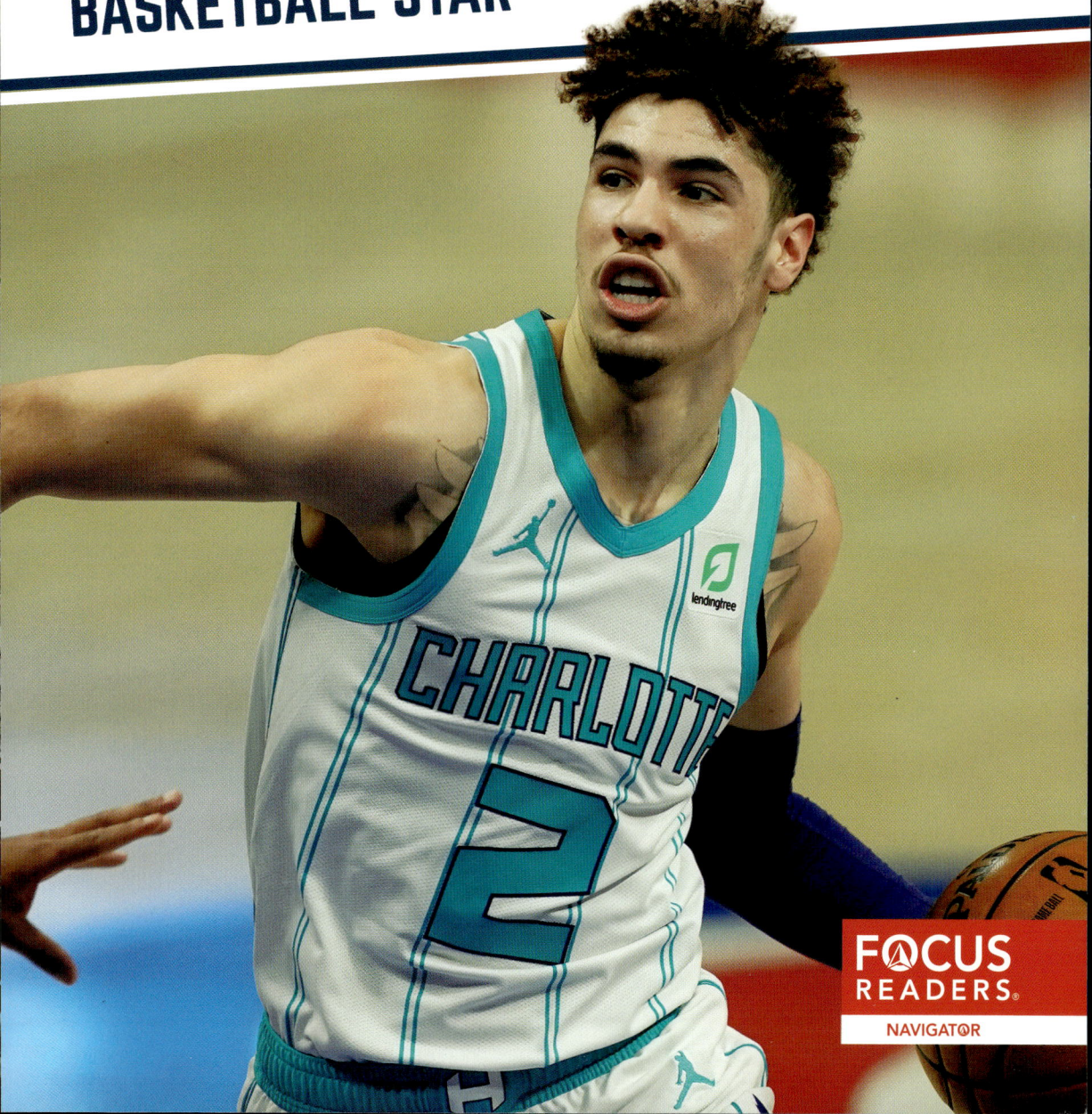

by Harold P. Cain

WWW.FOCUSREADERS.COM

Copyright © 2023 by Focus Readers®, Lake Elmo, MN 55042. All rights reserved. No part of this book may be reproduced or utilized in any form or by any means without written permission from the publisher.

Focus Readers is distributed by North Star Editions:
sales@northstareditions.com | 888-417-0195

Produced for Focus Readers by Red Line Editorial.

Photographs ©: Carlos Osorio/AP Images, cover, 1; Derick Hingle/AP Images, 4–5, 6, 9; Louis Lopez/Cal Sport Media/Zuma Wire/AP Images, 10–11, 13, 15; Mindaugas Kulbis/AP Images, 16–17; Liusjenas Kulbis/AP Images, 19; Rick Rycroft/AP Images, 21; Tony Dejak/AP Images, 22–23; Jacob Kupferman/AP Images, 25, 27; Red Line Editorial, 29

Library of Congress Cataloging-in-Publication Data
Names: Cain, Harold P., author.
Title: LaMelo Ball : basketball star / Harold P. Cain.
Description: Lake Elmo, MN : Focus Readers, [2023] | Series: Biggest names in sports | Includes index. | Audience: Grades 4-6
Identifiers: LCCN 2021055436 (print) | LCCN 2021055437 (ebook) | ISBN 9781637392539 (hardcover) | ISBN 9781637393055 (paperback) | ISBN 9781637394069 (pdf) | ISBN 9781637393574 (ebook)
Subjects: LCSH: Ball, LaMelo, 2001---Juvenile literature. | Basketball players--United States--Biography--Juvenile literature. | Charlotte Hornets (Basketball team : 2014-)--Juvenile literature.
Classification: LCC GV884.B26 C35 2023 (print) | LCC GV884.B26 (ebook) | DDC 796.323092 [B]--dc23/eng/20211220
LC record available at https://lccn.loc.gov/2021055436
LC ebook record available at https://lccn.loc.gov/2021055437

Printed in the United States of America
Mankato, MN
082022

ABOUT THE AUTHOR

Harold P. Cain is a retired English teacher and lifelong sports fan originally from Rockford, Illinois. He and his wife now live in Cathedral City, California, where they enjoy hiking, golf, and spending time with their daughter and three grandchildren in Los Angeles.

TABLE OF CONTENTS

CHAPTER 1

Family Reunion 5

CHAPTER 2

Ball Brothers 11

CHAPTER 3

Going Pro 17

CHAPTER 4

Arriving in the NBA 23

At-a-Glance Map • 28
Focus on LaMelo Ball • 30
Glossary • 31
To Learn More • 32
Index • 32

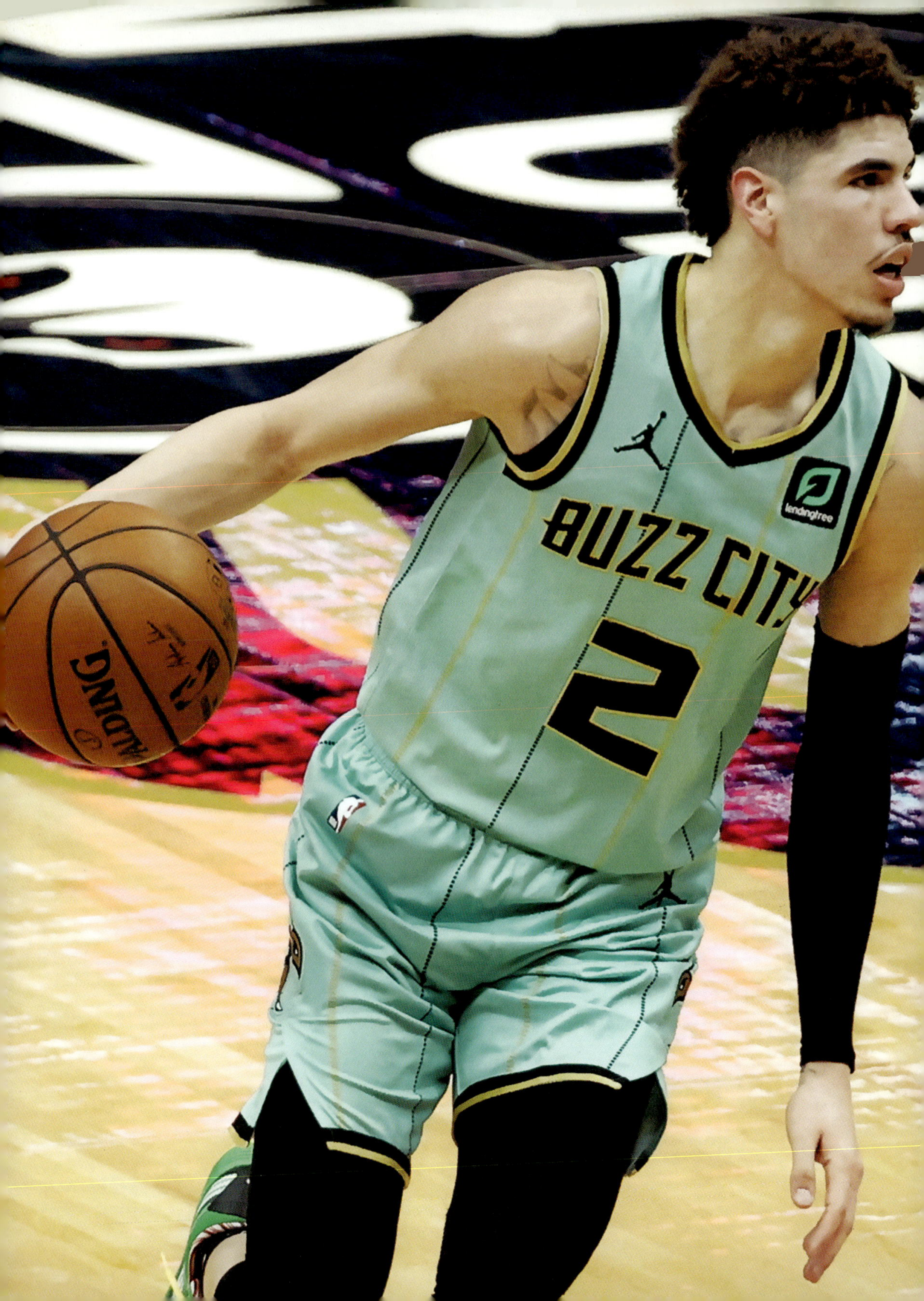
BUZZ CITY
2
SPALDING

CHAPTER 1

FAMILY REUNION

LaMelo Ball had been waiting all his life for this moment. He and the Charlotte Hornets were facing the New Orleans Pelicans on January 8, 2021. This wasn't a normal game for LaMelo. It was a family reunion. His older brother Lonzo was playing for the other team. It was the first competitive game the brothers had

LaMelo Ball dribbles the basketball during a 2021 game against the New Orleans Pelicans.

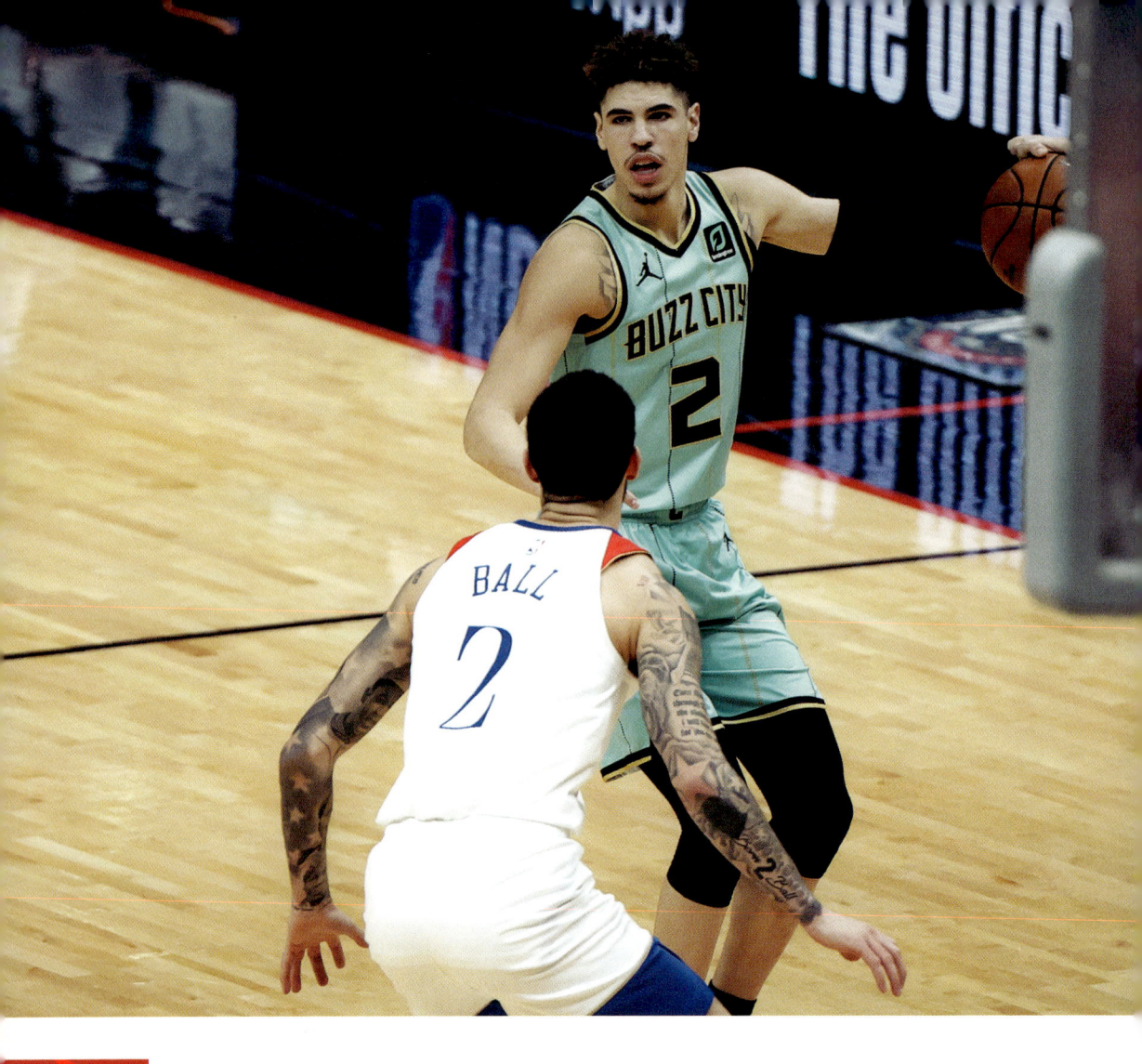

LaMelo (top) is guarded by his brother Lonzo in their first competitive game against each other.

ever played against each other. Their only other matchups had taken place at home when they were kids.

On this night, Lonzo was getting the best of LaMelo. New Orleans led by as many as 18 points in the second quarter. But LaMelo wasn't ready to give up just yet. In the third quarter, he faked a shot and drove toward the hoop. Then he dished a pass to Miles Bridges, who buried a three-pointer.

Later in the quarter, LaMelo dribbled to the three-point line. He faked a drive, but then he backed off. He put up an arcing shot over Lonzo. The ball hit nothing but net.

By the end of the third quarter, the Hornets were down by only five points. In the fourth, LaMelo found Gordon

Hayward for three. That shot gave the Hornets a four-point lead. Charlotte went on to win by a score of 118–110.

It was just the ninth game of LaMelo's career in the National Basketball Association (NBA). And he had just beaten his older brother. LaMelo's impressive stats were a big reason why. He finished the game with 12 points, 10 **rebounds** and 9 **assists**. He did that in only 25 minutes of action.

Just one more assist would have given LaMelo double digits in three categories. That's known as a triple-double. At the age of 19 years and 139 days, LaMelo would have been the youngest player ever

Ball drives to the basket as Pelicans players try to defend him.

to record a triple-double. He didn't have to wait long to set the record. He did it the very next day.

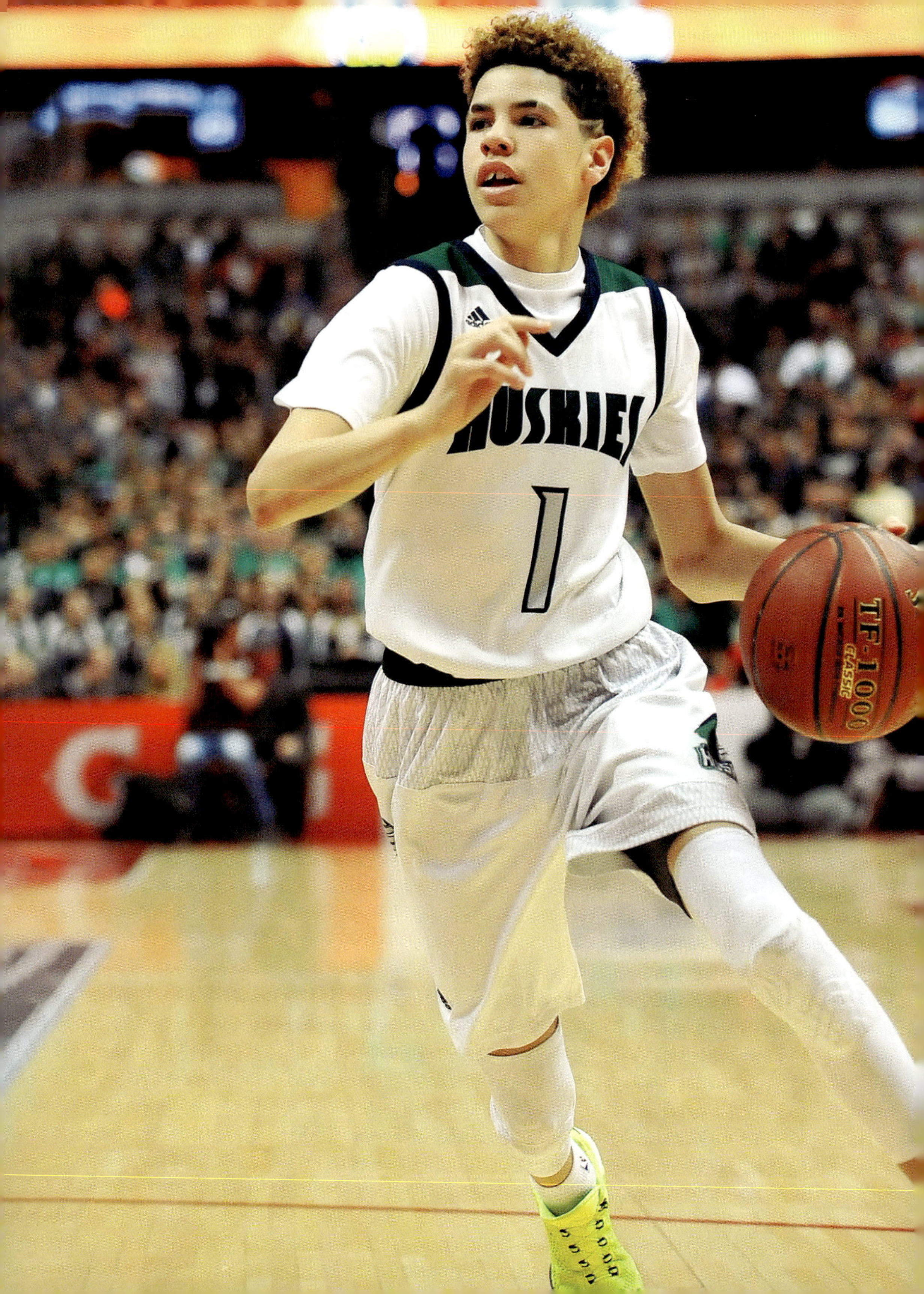
HUSKIES
1
TF-1000
CLASSIC

CHAPTER 2

BALL BROTHERS

LaMelo Ball was born on August 22, 2001. There was never any doubt about which sport he would play. His dad, LaVar, had been a college basketball player. His mom, Tina, also played college ball. His older brothers, Lonzo and LiAngelo, started playing almost as soon as they could walk. LaMelo was no

Fourteen-year-old LaMelo Ball competes in a high school game in March 2016.

different. LaVar was his first coach. Lonzo and LiAngelo were his first teammates. The brothers grew up playing together at their home in Southern California.

Starting in 2014, the Ball brothers began playing together on a team their

PRO BALLERS

All three Ball brothers went on to play pro basketball. The oldest brother, Lonzo, was the second overall pick in the 2017 NBA **Draft**. He began his career with the Los Angeles Lakers. In 2019, he joined the New Orleans Pelicans. And in 2021, he became a member of the Chicago Bulls. Meanwhile, LiAngelo played pro ball with minor league teams. As of 2021, he was still trying to earn a spot on an NBA team.

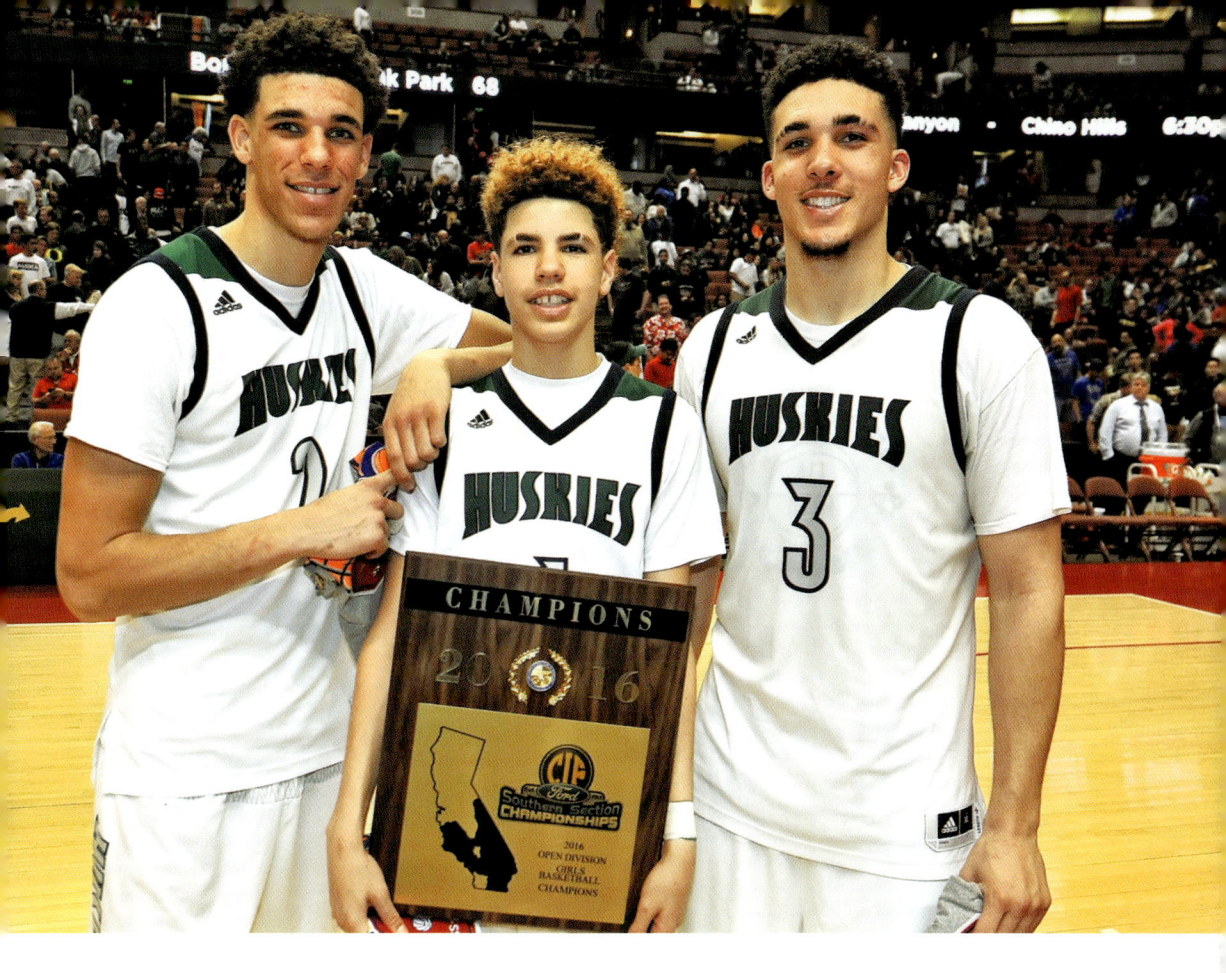

LaMelo (center) celebrates a state championship with his brothers in 2016.

father started. It was called Big Ballers VXT. The team was meant to be for high school players. LaMelo was only in seventh grade at the time. Even so, he was one of the best players on the team.

Like his brothers, LaMelo attended Chino Hills High School. LaMelo played **point guard** for the school's basketball team. He was great at running the offense. He could also score plenty of points. When LaMelo was still just 13, he racked up 27 points in his first game. Chino Hills had a perfect 35–0 record that season. LaMelo helped his team win the state championship.

The next year, LaMelo really stepped up his scoring ability. In one game, he put up 29 points by halftime. And he was only getting started. LaMelo scored 63 more in the second half. He had 41 points in the fourth quarter alone.

LaMelo leads Chino Hills during a 2017 game against Oak Hill Academy.

LaMelo was incredibly successful on the court. However, LaVar didn't think his son was being coached properly. For that reason, he pulled LaMelo out of school before his junior season. Where he played next came as a surprise to everyone.

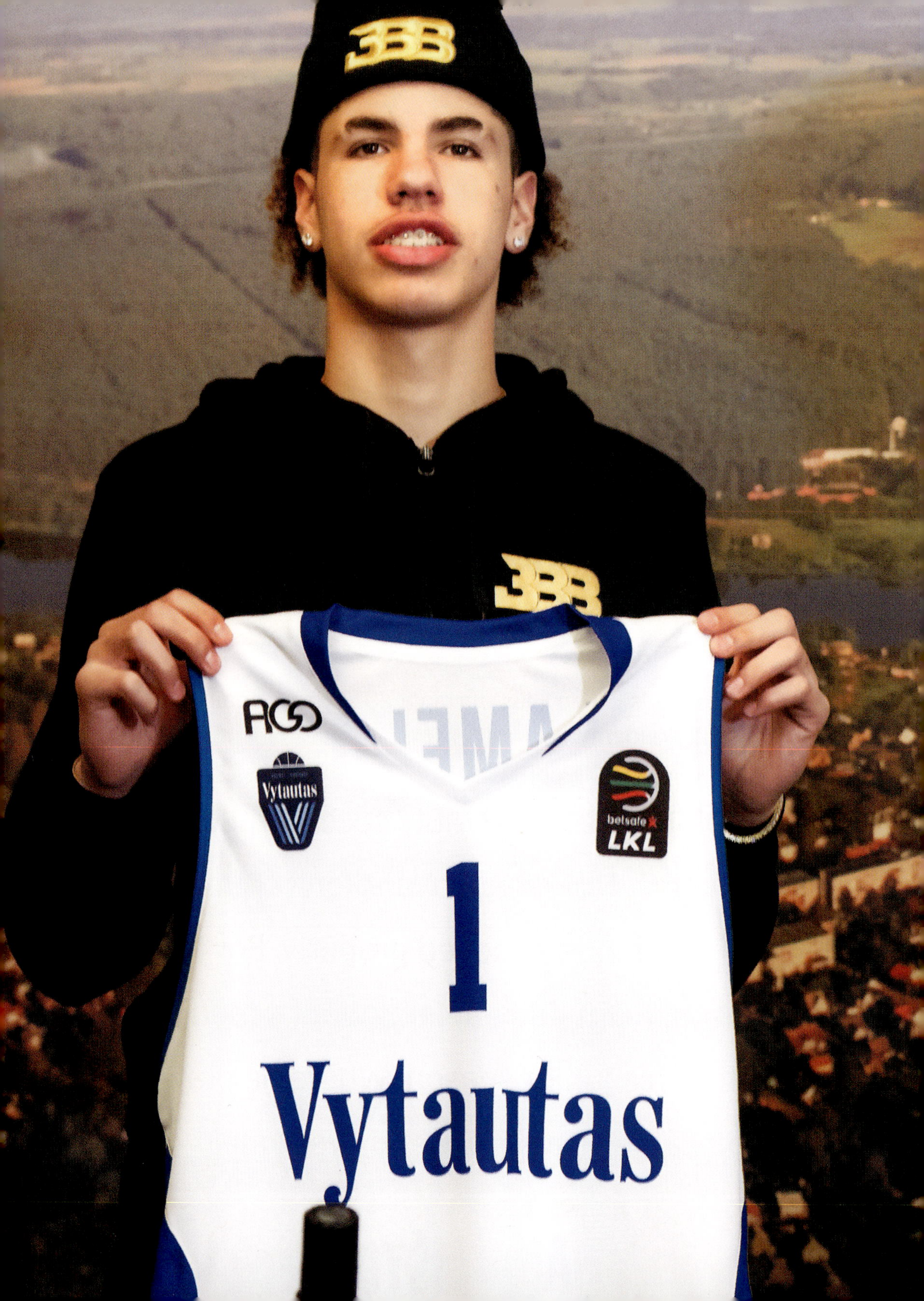
Vytautas
betsafe
LKL
1
Vytautas

CHAPTER 3

GOING PRO

Most **professional** basketball players go to college before entering the NBA. However, LaMelo Ball wasn't most players. At the age of 16, he went to Europe and became a pro. He signed with BC Vytautas in Lithuania. His brother LiAngelo signed with the team, too.

LaMelo Ball shows off his new jersey after signing a pro contract with a team in Europe.

LaMelo was the youngest American ever to sign a pro basketball **contract**. However, it was a challenging experience for him. For one thing, he didn't get much playing time. He averaged less than seven points per game. He also struggled with injuries. LaMelo and LiAngelo ended up leaving Lithuania before the season was over. Even so, LaMelo still learned a lot from his time in Europe.

His next step was much closer to home. LaMelo joined the Los Angeles Ballers of the Junior Basketball Association (JBA). LaVar Ball had created the JBA as an alternative to college basketball. LaMelo averaged nearly 40 points per game.

LaMelo plays in a 2018 game with Lithuanian team BC Vytautas.

After the JBA season ended, LaMelo returned to high school. He chose to play his senior season at SPIRE Institute in Ohio. He played with other top college **prospects**. LaMelo was one of the best

19

young players the United States. However, he had already played pro basketball. For that reason, it wasn't clear if he would be allowed to play college ball. So, LaMelo decided he was turning pro for good.

He wasn't quite ready for the NBA, though. Instead, he signed with the Illawarra Hawks in Australia. LaMelo

BIG BALLER BRAND

Most basketball players don't get sneakers named after them until they reach the NBA. But LaMelo's dad owned a shoe company. It was called Big Baller Brand. In 2017, the company released the Melo Ball 1. LaMelo was only 16 at the time. That made him the youngest athlete to have his own sneaker.

LaMelo Ball takes part in a 2019 game with the Illawarra Hawks in Australia.

proved he was much more prepared for the pros than he had been in Europe. In one game, he became the youngest player in league history to record a triple-double. And at the end of the season, he was named **Rookie** of the Year. LaMelo had taken an unusual path. But now he was ready for the NBA.

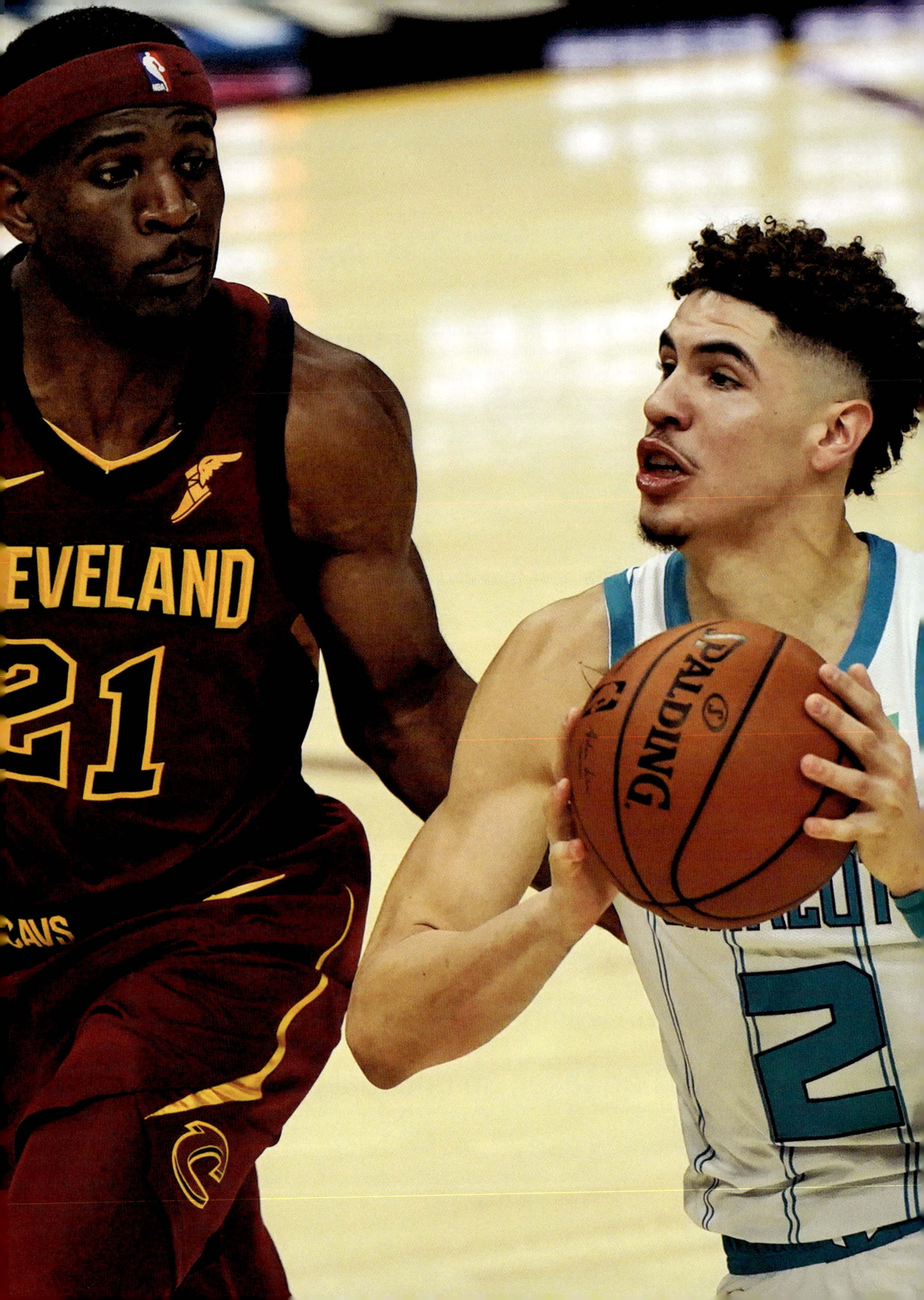
EVELAND
21
CAVS
SPALDING
2

CHAPTER 4

ARRIVING IN THE NBA

The Charlotte Hornets chose LaMelo Ball third overall in the 2020 NBA Draft. And when the 2020–21 season arrived, Ball got off to a fast start. One early highlight came when he faced off against his brother Lonzo for the first time. He didn't quite notch a triple-double

LaMelo Ball drives past a defender in December 2020 during his first NBA game.

in that game. But one night later, he got it done.

Ball and the Hornets faced the Atlanta Hawks on January 9, 2021. Ball was nearly unstoppable. He hit 9 of his 13 shots. He also recorded 12 rebounds and 11 assists. One of his assists came on a behind-the-back pass to set up a teammate for a three-pointer. At the age of 19 years and 140 days, Ball became the youngest NBA player ever to record a triple-double.

Ball won Rookie of the Month in the first three months of the season. In February, he broke out with his best scoring performance yet. Against the

Ball makes a no-look pass against the Atlanta Hawks in January 2021.

Utah Jazz, Ball scored a career-high 34 points. Most impressively, he made shots from all over the court. He hit step-back threes. He also made full-court drives to the hoop. Ball averaged more than 20 points per game in February.

The only thing that could slow him down was an injury. Ball broke his wrist in a March game. At the time, he was leading all rookies in assists and steals. He was second in scoring.

Ball came back for the last few games of the season. In all, he played in only 51 games. However, he still managed to lead all rookies in assists and steals.

SOCIAL MEDIA STAR

LaMelo Ball became a popular player at a young age. Before he had even played in an NBA game, he had more social media followers than many NBA players. In fact, Ball's Instagram account was more popular than those of some NBA teams. By the end of 2021, Ball had more than seven million Instagram followers.

Ball throws down a monster dunk against the Indiana Pacers during the 2021–22 season.

When the season ended, Ball was named Rookie of the Year. Hornets fans hoped it wouldn't be long before he led the team to the playoffs.

AT-A-GLANCE MAP

LAMELO BALL

- Height: 6 feet 6 inches (198 cm)
- Weight: 180 pounds (82 kg)
- Birth date: August 22, 2001
- Birthplace: Anaheim, California
- High schools: Chino Hills High School (Chino Hills, California); SPIRE Institute (Geneva, Ohio)
- Minor league teams: BC Vytautas (2018); Los Angeles Ballers (2018); Illawarra Hawks (2019–20)
- NBA team: Charlotte Hornets (2020–)
- Major awards: NBA Rookie of the Year (2021)

Los Angeles | Anaheim | Chino Hills | Geneva | Charlotte

Prienai

Wollongong

FOCUS ON
LAMELO BALL

Write your answers on a separate piece of paper.

1. Write a sentence that describes the key idea of Chapter 2.

2. Do you think Ball should have gone to college instead of becoming a pro right away? Why or why not?

3. What team were the Hornets playing when Ball became the youngest NBA player to score a triple-double?

    A. Atlanta Hawks
    B. New Orleans Pelicans
    C. Utah Jazz

4. Why didn't Ball score many points when he played in Lithuania?

    A. He had more playing time than in high school.
    B. He struggled with injuries and didn't play much.
    C. The Lithuanian league had different rules.

Answer key on page 32.

GLOSSARY

assists
Passes that lead directly to a teammate scoring a basket.

contract
An agreement to pay someone a certain amount of money.

draft
A system that allows teams to acquire new players coming into a league.

point guard
The player on a basketball team who runs the team's offense.

professional
Paid to do something as a job, rather than doing it just for fun.

prospects
Players who are likely to be successful in the future.

rebounds
Plays in which a player controls the ball after a missed shot.

rookie
A professional athlete in his or her first year.

TO LEARN MORE

BOOKS

Doeden, Matt. *Basketball Greats*. North Mankato, MN: Capstone Press, 2022.

Gigliotti, Jim. *Charlotte Hornets*. Mankato, MN: The Child's World, 2019.

Walker, Hubert. *Ja Morant: Basketball Star*. Lake Elmo, MN: Focus Readers, 2021.

NOTE TO EDUCATORS

Visit **www.focusreaders.com** to find lesson plans, activities, links, and other resources related to this title.

INDEX

Atlanta Hawks, 24

Ball, LaVar, 11–13, 15, 18, 20
Ball, LiAngelo, 11–12, 17–18
Ball, Lonzo, 5–8, 11–12, 23
Ball, Tina, 11
Big Ballers VXT, 13
Bridges, Miles, 7

Charlotte Hornets, 5–9, 23–27
Chicago Bulls, 12
Chino Hills High School, 14

Hayward, Gordon, 7–8

Illawarra Hawks, 20

Junior Basketball Association (JBA), 18–19

Los Angeles Ballers, 18
Los Angeles Lakers, 12

New Orleans Pelicans, 5–8, 12

SPIRE Institute, 19

Utah Jazz, 25

Vytautas, 17–18

Answer Key: 1. Answers will vary; 2. Answers will vary; 3. A; 4. B